Near Hits and Lost Classics

Near Hits and Lost Classics

Early Poems by

Quincy R. Lehr

Cover design by Shay Culligan

ISBN: 978-1-952326-93-6

Kelsay Books
502 South 1040 East, A-119
American Fork, Utah, 84003

For Sarah Lundberg and Ray Pospisil

Also by Quincy R. Lehr

William Montgomery (EXOT/Modern Metrics, 2006)

Across the Grid of Streets (Seven Towers, 2008)

William Montgomery's Guide to New York City
    (Seven Towers, 2008/DYAD, 2017)

Obscure Classics of English Progressive Rock
    (Seven Towers, 2012)

Shadows and Gifts (Barefoot Muse Press, 2013)

Heimat (Barefoot Muse Press, 2014)

The Dark Lord of the Tiki Bar (Measure Press, 2015)

Foreword

I have, for or better or worse, reached a point where I can speak of my "early period," defined in the main by the books that Seven Towers published in Dublin between 2008 and 2012. This book represents a fairly generous selection of the two Seven Towers full-lengthers, *Across the Grid of Streets* (2008) and *Obscure Classics of English Progressive Rock* (2012), as well as the entirety of the 2008 mini-book, *William Montgomery's Guide to New York City,* the last of which saw a small-scale re-release in 2017 from Montreal's DYAD Press. But what other than being associated with a particular publisher and being written when I was younger than I am now makes these poems "early"?

In the first place, going back though the work, I find I engage with it differently than with my more recent collections. It's not that different from finding a photograph from a long-ended relationship—one can *recall* the emotion without *reliving* it, or wanting to relive it. Can I write a better poem than "The Joke" or "A Certain Point of View"? I should goddamn well hope so! But I'll never write *those poems* again, find myself in the same set of circumstances—a mélange of expatriation and repatriation, loss, sorrow, and... unexpected pleasures during and after a series of life-altering events.

As such, I wasn't particularly tempted to mess with the poems much, save to move around a bit of punctuation, fix the occasional metrical hiccough, do a bit of obvious and discrete wording improvement, and the like. At this point, the poems are more or less in their definitive state. I am surprised at how many of my early poems I still like. The ones I don't like are gone. I doubt anyone will miss "Continental Drift"—my first foray into the heavily allusive longer poem, as was a bit too obvious. Nor do I suspect that those already familiar with *Obscure Classics* will bemoan the absence of the frankly miserablist "Triptych" with its strained Biblical metaphor. I could go on in this manner for a bit, as the expunged poems, while a minority of the whole, aren't a negligible minority, but suffice it to say that I doubt I'm alone by finding my earlier work more agreeable with a bit less of it on hand.

Revisiting this material also reminds me that one's early work mostly flies the flag, staking out claims and launching initial forays into territory that probably isn't as virgin as one thinks it is, but is nevertheless new to the author. "The Joke," sprawling and possibly overstuffed as it is, is an obvious precursor to *Heimat*, especially with Ernst Lehr making an early appearance. (I have since learned his fairly prosaic fate—I like the versions I imagined better.) On the other hand, while the more straightforwardly autobiographical "Time Zones" is somewhat unusual for me, being an attempt to write a verse autobiography to get that impulse at least partly out of my system, its uniqueness gives it a certain charm, at least for me.

I owe many people a great deal for having a poetic "career," or whatever one calls being in the position of generally being able to find avenues of publication and a modest readership for one's work. In particular, though, back in 2007, Sarah Lundberg saw something in the work of a fish-out-of-water American with (at the time) a pretty modest list of publication credits and few connections that made her want to publish those books. Sarah was not always the easiest person in the world to get along with, and God knows I'm not, either, but her early support was crucial.

—Quincy R. Lehr
Los Angeles, CA

Contents

from *Obscure Classics of English Progressive Rock* (2012)

from *Across the Grid of Streets* (2008)

A shot rang out

Most nights, I drown the city noises out,
Treating them like faint, abrasive Musak,
A fugue of drunken rants and engines belching
With little variation. Three floors up,
I'm well above the murmurs on the block—
The idle youths with baggy jeans and forties
Who smoke their menthol cigarettes and smirk,
The withered wino wrapped around the stoop,
A groaning concierge who asks for change
As tenants stagger in on Friday nights.

But not so long ago, some drunken prick
Opened fire on the building's stairwell
With booze and Spanish curses on his breath—
An angry shit with bloodlust and bad aim.
He's just another pissed Dominican—
A sketch the cops taped on a corner lamppost,
Decked out with bling and a dull, reptilian stare,
A wanted poster, someone else's problem.
It's not my business, after all—although
The stairs are only paces from my door.

The shot went wild, and someone called the cops,
Whose knocks rang out like flails of heavy truncheons
Against my bolted door. Their questions barked
Like orders when they asked me if I'd heard
Something unusual that night. I blinked,
Pointed to my pajamas, and said no.
In moments, they declared me innocent
Of shooting—and of calling 911.

I smoked a cigarette, then went to bed,
Still grumbling at the minutes lost to dreams.
When morning came, I felt like I had failed,
Grown jaded and uncaring, with each lock,
Each buzzer, and each key a talisman
Of chosen and indifferent isolation.
It's all too much sometimes—the paper cups
With jangling change, the noises from the street
Exhaling threats, malt liquor, and stale smoke.
I slept through gunfire just outside my door.

A letter home

The sound comes in a burble from the street,
Strained, like the words you mumble through a pillow.
Cast against the headlights, clots of cloud
Hang low and gray—inert—until they billow
To fill the black of sky. And lurching feet
Plod up the stairs, intermittent, loud.

An old and musty building with a view
Of an unknown steeple set in solemn lines—
This is where I live. The music's off,
And there's no soundtrack to the chokes and whines
Of traffic trundling in a rumbling queue,
Except, perhaps, my ragged smoker's cough.

"Georgian Dublin" rots in constant damp,
The way it always has, I guess—although
Only weeks have passed since I moved in,
And I'm in no position yet to know
The letter from the flashy postage stamp:
Which decay comes from without—which from within.

A sense of some exquisite isolation
Permeates this hour. The neighborhood,
With "Joycean" connotations, does not know
That I'm right here, and even if it could
Direct its gaze at me—my transplantation
To these shores—would it merely show

That I'm another graft, like Polish signs
In windows—or reality TV
On screens in pubs? Or the taco shells I bought?
Or that whole tourist crap facsimile
Of the "Ould Sod" in D2 shops where lines
Of visitors throw down the cash they brought

To pay the piper on Grafton Street? I'll stop
Complaining, since the rain remains outside,
Falling, as it does most every day,
To form a slick of moisture as I hide
Behind my window, staring at each drop
Just outside, yet a continent away.

A certain point of view

Take an errant strand of hair
And hold it to the mirror.
Observe the shots of gray
That will not go away.
Your vaguely sunken chest is bare.
The warning sign is clearer.
No signal of distress
Will spring you from this mess.

You got the girlfriend, took the job
But swore that you were missing
The promise of a dream,
And soon enough the team
Dismissed you to the bench to sob
Your useless reminiscing
That might as well be true.
A certain point of view

Refracts the truth like spectacles
Bend light to aid eyes' weakness.
That aching in the wrist,
That winsome girl you kissed
Who grabbed you by the testicles
And forced you into meekness…
Was it all a lie
That led to that good-bye?

Some men marry; some do not
And sleepwalk through their lives
Half-dressed with noses filled with snot
And glares for those with wives.

She kissed you in the parking lot
And whispered in a stammer
Of things that people do,
And after it was through,
You wished there was a second shot
In timing or in grammar.
But no, there's no such luck,
And so you pass the buck

To parents, preachers, passers-by,
The economic system,
Your current state of health—
Or current lack of wealth.
The constant silence of the sky
Reminds you that you missed them:
The one-off shots at fame,
The season-clinching game.

But life goes on like TV shows
Re-run on basic cable
Past any relevance.
The pesky present tense
Will melt like February snows
Seen from the kitchen table.
The spring comes like a bet
Left uncollected yet.

But dreams sustain us like a pill,
And so we dream and hope
To fight off bouts of getting ill
With mantras used like dope.

Why there is no socialism in the United States of America

At 4:15 AM, the city bus
Had pulled up to the curb, its silhouette
Marked dimly by the light that crept through grates,
Fencing in empty stores. I paid my fare
And squeezed beside a sleepy Barnard girl.
She moved a centimeter to her left—
Away from me—and twitched a pinkish nose
Below gray, narrowed eyes, accusing me
Of *something,* so I leaned against the glass
And stared at greasy, distant streaks of light.

Each one of us was tired, pissed-off, and bored,
Angry at the hour and with those pricks—
That fat-assed bitch, who muttered at a cell phone,
That rat-faced airline worker at the front,
That punk-ass hoodlum, glaring at his feet,
That stuck-up twat, that sad-eyed brown-haired schmuck
Gawking at New York's predawn, backlit blackness.
And if we were united, our disdain
For every dumbshit creep—in short, ourselves—
Had fused our isolations into one.

Alternative rock song

Drunker with each snifter downed
    And older by the minute,
You wonder where the trouble lies
    Despite your drowning in it.
The stereo is up-to-date
    And blares out the Replacements,
Returning you to summer days
    You spent bombed out in basements.

This is the alternative,
    The hipster's rise to favor,
The halcyon year of jubilee
    The Alpha and Omega.

The girl's stacked up with silicone,
    A batshit crazy boozer.
She'll ride you raw with expertise
    As long as you amuse her.
The lounge is laced with ecstasy;
    She fumbles with your britches
And tracks the furrows other girls
    Had dug in blue-jean ditches.

This is the alternative,
    The advertising's target.
An angry generation still
    Spends money on the market.

An earring and a sticker on
    The bumper of a Lexus
Mark a demographic, an
    Expansion of the nexus.
There's punk rock on the radio,
    On cell phones and commercials.
There's punk rock in your hard-on, though
    It's seeing some reversals.

This is the alternative
    To starched-up, stuck-up culture.
It dominates the boardroom like
    An avant-gardist sculpture.

A dream home heartache? Not so fast!
    You never were quite vice-less.
The salary is 80K—
    The attitude is priceless.
A plutocrat in rented rooms,
    An erstwhile hand at protest—
Back on the wagon for a while
    So you can pass your drug test.

This is the alternative.
    The children raise their voices
In choruses learned from TV sets
    Insinuating choices.

It's all just work

An urban yokel slack-jaw yawn
Came belching from behind his teeth
At curses of graffiti scrawl
While drifts of garbage spread beneath
The train like shrapnel. Just past dawn,
Commuters winced at the subway's squall
While powdered sugar caked a sleeve
And the caffeine kicked in. Time to leave.

The train ride ended, and the walk
To crowded offices was fast,
To blinking screens and new accounts
Of someone else's money. Past
The back-and-forth of aimless talk
And shuffling of the screens' amounts,
The crowds were settling to a hush
An hour beyond the sugar rush.

The pitch was weak,
But the ball's in play
For the five-day week
And the eight-hour day,
For the two-week trip
To a distant land
For a big, fat tip
From the cash in hand.

And in the evening, sheets of sweat
Clung like cologne to pallid flesh
Cooked gray by sallow lights indoors.
A change of clothes, and all was fresh
Or something like it, but the wet
Of thwarted yearning leaked through pores
And spoiled that briefly polished air
A new shirt short of debonair.

She felt no better, and her face
Relaxed in mute acceptance, bit
The rubbed-off lipstick of a smirk
As if to stop a laughing fit,
Then forced her mouth back into place.
She muttered, "Well, it's all just work,"
Then settled on an absent grin,
Her mouth locked tight and eyes fenced in.

The joints will creak,
And your eyes will say
That the flesh is weak,
But the soul's okay.
Still, the tongue will trip,
And the words you planned
Jumble up and slip
Like a groping hand.

The joke

The Universe is the Practical Joke of the General
    at the Expense of the Particular, quoth FRATER
    PERDURABO, and laughed....
But though FRATER PERDURABO laughed
    openly, He also at the same time wept secretly;
    and in Himself He neither laughed nor wept.
Nor did He mean what He said.
                              —Aleister Crowley

I

But if the general is just a joke
At something more particular's expense,
And if I rarely glimpse the thing through smoke
And wavering shadows, should I trust my sense?
Beyond this room, these off-white walls, that door
With bolted locks, the outside's notional,
Pastiched from knee-jerk hunches at its core.
    Let's not get too emotional,

Since if I don't quite mean the things I say
Or don't know why I mean them, it's not spite
Or purred mendacity that sets the way
The syllables escape.
                              Off-yellow light
Shone on stacks of books, their pages dog-eared,
Bent covers, old receipts that held a place
In arguments I'd set aside—and feared—
    That wrote themselves across my face.

And what if wisdom and some demiurge
Commingled sheepishly in lust and greed,
Their offspring much too powerful to purge
Or interdict? Would that explain this need

28

To grapple with uncertainty, to seek
A wobble in an orbit, to destroy
Our cautious symmetries, the words in Greek
   Embattled theories still employ,

Though with a stutter and a sidelong glance
At smirking wisdom—beatific, smug,
And whispering venom: "Life comes down to chance.
It's sperm and eggs, a vague genetic tug,
And rapid calculations—you're lost without
My guidance in your hurdle back to loam,
That race you run, not sure what it's about,
   To find that moving target, home."

If each piece has a place, who makes the chart
On which a blind cartographer plots out
The whole in which we try to place each part,
Our fingers trembling, measurements in doubt?
Yes, I have mapped it out before, and smirked,
Hiding in wounded sentiment.
                         I've sworn
Oaths with fingers crossed, and been reborn,
Only to age again.
              It's never worked.
The coasts stay squiggles, and my resolution
To fill the empty inland spaces falters—
Chalk it up to a fragile constitution;
Offer it up in prayers at gilded altars.

II

The lights were coming on as I approached
The concrete steps that climbed to reach her door,
Flickering beneath me as I stopped
And raised my hand to knock.
                              The subjects broached,
As always, were implicit, as we swore
The same tired oaths to causes long since dropped
Due to fatigue and truculent events,
To finer furniture and higher rents.

And her lips locked,   then lifted an answer
From a fragmented phrase   she found in a book
By a lapsed leftist   beloved by her set,
A Gallophile ignored   (save in grumbles) by mine.
Semiotics and ale,   amber-dark,
Tinted our talk,   which teetered and fell
Like bleated "buts"   that broke from a sentence
Unsaid and silly.   I sighed and coughed,
Then rushed from the rasp   of her roughened voice,
Sanded by the smoke   of her cigarettes.
And I walked outside,
Letting the music propel me from the apartment

And onto the balcony, and I stared at the neighborhood,
Where the gray stray cat languidly eyed the squirrel
    preoccupied with a stray candy wrapper,
Where the middle manager in cotton-polyester blend khaki pants
    jacked off in his Lexus at the stop sign
    while the classic rock station blared out "Radar Love,"

which he tried to hum atonally as he neared climax,
Where the leaves of low trees between the roofs
    dappled the couple walking their dog
    with driblets of shadow,
Where memories, like ambiguous messiahs,
    became flesh and dwelt among us,

And I flipped a coin—
Heads I stay. Tails I go.
It was at that moment that night began,
That the dust on the window sill became invisible,
That the lights in backyards swarmed like fireflies around a
    barbecue.

—

Kitchen chairs. A window to the yard.
Weeds among the flowers I disregard.
Rotting porch. A jigsaw of gray slats.
Philosophies enshrined on welcome mats.
A sizzling pulse on fire from ephedrine.
Waiting for fatigue to scrape me clean.

Girl's long gone. Cigarette hand is shaking.
Mind erupts with points I should be making.
Power lines. Low-slung cyclone fences.
Dime-store speed caressing weary senses.
Anger abates. Beginnings of erection.
Should I call her? "Always use protection."

Cat meows. Startled crickets scatter.
Coursing thoughts in tones of radio chatter.
Queasy gut. Dirty, empty plate.
Distant noises from the interstate.
Cup of coffee. Jolt and palpitation.
Breathless, I review the situation.

Album plays. It's still *A Globe of Frogs*.
Soft guitar and barks of neighbors' dogs.
Phone's inert. A synapse spits her number.
4 AM. Anticipated slumber.
Up three days—eyes shiver, nose is runny.
At the edge of sleep, it all seems pretty funny.

III

Fame's poor relation, faux-prophetic hack
On stage in some dank bar and telling jokes.
They laugh, but *at* you when you turn your back
Or when they head outside for furtive smokes.
Ethnic white, slicked hair, a sagging paunch—
A "great career" that somehow failed to launch.

A thousand stand-up comics spat their acts
At paying customers, who only stared
And laughed politely at the eager faces
Up on stage. Some songs should not be blared;
Some thoughts should stay unuttered; and some facts
Should be suppressed. "You fuckers take your places."

But wait! I think I saw you at Mylae!
But wait! Do you recall the fatal Ides?
The turning, turning falcon in the sky?
An empty tomb? The subtly changing tides?
Once man, once woman… does *that* ring a bell?
It doesn't? Not at all, you say? Oh well.

He wrapped his mouth around the mike
  And had them all in stitches
As if they'd never seen his like.
  "Now listen up you bitches…"

The easy laughs came quickly to the throat.
The easy targets struck, he paused to gloat…

But if the general is just a joke
At something more particular's expense,
And if our laughter strangles sentiment,
The punch-line gives pathetic recompense,
Malice in some comic "masterstroke,"
A smile belying murderous intent.

———

But evening traffic moves outside and winds
Across the grid of streets, until the thread
Reaches Katie, staring through the blinds
Of an upstairs window. She's sitting on her bed,
Vaguely waiting for a husband, who
Is doubtless caught in gridlock's tangled knots.
Restless, bored, with nothing else to do,
She loses herself in soaps and whiskey shots.

But did she say how well she did in school?
How handsome the man she married was, how long
It took to recognize him for a fool,
To realize how badly things went wrong?
She can remember walks along the river.
The morning tingled in glints upon the water.
He pulled her close, caressing every shiver—
Then married her and soon enough forgot her.

Now this—the Cuisinart, the high-heeled shoe
Balancing by a strap snagged on the night stand,
The TV in the living room, the view
Of houses just like hers, the contraband
Furtively smoked or snorted, and a maid
Who steals the silverware. Inebriate,
She wanders up and down the stairs, afraid
Of something she can name, but can't quite state.

O shine on Katie, doleful sinking sun!
Shine on the roof and the garden and the street!
Clothe her in light, though the day is almost done,
And though the colors are making their retreat
Into watchful grey, and though tired spouses
In columns of cars are winding their way back
To pills in the bathrooms of two-storey houses
That gird against another heart attack.

Alarms go on and off throughout the night
In lieu of movement, a faint cacophony
Of whoops and trills—with even, flashing light
Punctuating the quiet mystery

Of bleak suburban silence
And fantasies of violence
And the hidden sheen of chestnut hair
And a slip that leaves her shoulders bare
As she rolls over, carrying drapes of sheet
In an unconscious coil around her feet.

IV

A Lutheran reverend, born in Illinois,
Keeps his voice at an even pitch
And feigns a look of joy,
Son of a pastor, son of a bitch,

Through his Sunday sermon
One drizzle-speckled day in '17.
He speaks his father's German,
And the clerical collar's clean,

But grace is unbelieved, unsought
As Roland tugs at Gertrude's hair,
A newborn and a toddler, caught
Under their father's reproving stare.

Forced to the cloth by his family name,
Held to it by the fidgeting children—
Not to mention a sense of shame
At chafing at doing as he was bidden.

Always the "good son" who followed requests—
No prodigals in these here parts.
A charming wife and a house fit for guests
But this is where the trouble starts…

Honor thy father and thy mother—
Cram for exams in all-night sessions.
Marry your wife and covet no other.
Ensure that your children learn the right lessons.

Bored shepherd, staring through the glass
Of chapel windows and into a field,
His smile and sermons so much gas—
Which he hopes he can keep concealed.

But looking at the calm, brown eyes
Of his wife and children, he'd sometimes soften.
His faith would surge, to his surprise—
Though now that happens far less often.

(And cannons echoed through the night
As mud congealed around the dead,
Putrefying in line of sight
A continent away. The tread
Of feet in flapping boots, the stare
Of vacant eyes from a shattered head
Held the attention of Pastor Lehr—
Who only read about it then,
But must have dreamt of graves in France
And sloughing off his mortal skin—

Such a negation of permanence,
Respect, and duty! Such a way
To sink in anonymity—
A cipher dead in Flanders clay—
Leaving Grandpa, my father, me.)

The text is preached, and for an instant
A silence grips the farmers in the pews,
Soon broken by a screaming infant.

His wife's face screws
Into an apprehensive look.
She clasps her son's pink, squirming fingers.
The pastor flinches, shuts the book.
Hymnals open; the shrieking lingers.

So many Sundays spent preserving
The stolid souls of rustic Krauts;
Modest, decent, and undeserving—
Who wouldn't just get out?
But his eyes fix on his wife,
And he sighs at her dark-eyed beauty.
And he thinks about his life,
And he thinks about his duty—

Then cut to rain outside and burps of thunder
And gravestones slicked with wet.
"Hier stehe ich, ich kann nicht ander."
Wanna fucking bet?

—

A blank space on a map. A smallish town.
An outfit that just misses buttoned-down.
An academic robe. A framed degree.
Another way of saying "look at me."

A cigarette. "Make it a Manhattan."
Two sets of books. The thin one's for the tax man.
Prodigal son makes good. Reunion's set.
Sisters line up, and Mother's eyes are wet.

More drinks. No guest. The staff are growing bored.
A parking lot. Accelerator's floored.
Entrance ramp. Driving almost blind.
Remnants of the family stay behind.

Rammed brakes shriek. Disaster is averted.
A drink is downed. A phrase remains unblurted.
An unknown soldier molders in the loam.
A murdered bastard never made it home.

                              V

Where are we now?
                    It's difficult to say—
Somewhere between late March and early May,
Between the thaw beneath a sheet of ice
And ice's breaking.

              No offers of advice
Or comfort can relieve us as we wait,
Suspended, in transition from one state
Into another. Snowfall turns to rain
And freezes to a sheet of ice again.

How do we cope?
                The answer's been obscured
By doubtful forecasts and an unsaid word—
Or if it's uttered, the clouds all turn to smoke
In the obfuscating cover of a joke.

"Yeah, what've you been smoking, prick?
  Shut up and pass it this way.
I swear! You make me fucking sick.
  For God's sake, it's a Friday."

The film of grease that slicked across his face
Met globs of sweat descending from his hair,
Viscous with mousse. His strutting, violent pace

Across the stage disturbed the fetid air,
Tingling and toxic in each grasping throat.
His bald spot caught the light and seared each stare.

He sipped his water, tossed aside his coat,
Revealing sweat stains soaking through his shirt
And inching toward his tie. He seemed to gloat—

Not knowing that the fundamental hurt
That pained us into laughter didn't flow
Out of his armpits or his mouth, his spurt

39

Of crass and bigoted invective. No,
Such laughter as there was had come unbidden
From somewhere well outside his tawdry show

Upon that tawdry stage. Its source was hidden
Within the wounds he bore on entering,
That pain, fatigue, and alcohol had ridden

To crisis points, to punch lines that would sting—
And might perhaps—perhaps not—mean a thing.

VI

In feeding troughs of cafeterias,
In shrieks of a soprano's arias,
In an SUV, speeding toward a church,
In the weaving steps of a singing drunkard's lurch,
In a polysyllabic list of ingredients,
Crammed in between the myrrh and frankincense,
   You have to know the joke by now.

In sophistries of a seasoned charlatan,
In a politician's reckless battle plan,
In protest marches never caught on tape,
In the frantic, gibbering mouth of the "sapient ape,"
In this and that or some damn other thing,
In mouths that chatter, in the hands that cling,
   You have to know the joke by now.

And I shrugged it off.
Thanks, guys, you're too much.
There's the door. Do keep in touch.
And I laughed at the implications of the radio reports
   and the constant stream of traffic
   and the befuddled look on her face
And at the shotgun weddings and the sobbing lovers
   and the jilted sentiments of innocence curdling in that merciless
      sun
   that sustains and wrinkles us all
And at „Ein Feste Burg" and the Krak des Chevaliers falling into
      ruin
   and the photographs in the bottoms of boxes,
And at Will Rogers, who never met a man he didn't like.
And if the general is just a joke
At something more particular's expense…

Since if I don't quite mean the things I say
Or don't know why I mean them, it's not spite…

But it all comes down to the rain
That raineth every day,
And the things we don't exactly mean to say
—*Sir Bones: Henry's mad againe.*

And the Mississippi flows south
Past Minnesota farmland
And the brick and rust of declining Illinois industrial towns
And that utterly pointless arch in St Louis
And the generic bustle of Memphis
And the famous name of Vicksburg

And past Baton Rouge
Until it reaches the corrupted, mildewed hulk of New Orleans…
Jazz and heat and a thousand miles of run-off…
But it's *cold* up here—
And was there ever a city as useless as Minneapolis?

But wait, I think I saw you at Mylae!
But wait, I think…!
                 I think…
                       I think…
                             I think…

Such negation of permanence!
   You have to know the joke by now.
Shut up and pass it this way…
A thousand stand-up comics spat their acts
At paying customers…

No, wait! I think…
                 I think…
('Complexion Latin')
                       I think…
(Son of a pastor, son of a bitch)
                             I think…

And the thoughts flow together into a morass of punch-lines,
   of set-ups and sight gags and a chorus line of incoherent
      scatting…
   turn, turn, kick, turn…
And half-remembered lines of poetry and missed buses
   and that crazy woman on the train…

But still

There's the acclaim and the raree show and the powder against
          sweat
    and the tawdry bulbs around dressing-room mirrors
    where tawdry fans wait in expectation
And there's a woman halfway across the room
    and you're trying to maneuver yourself
    into her line of sight (turn, turn, kick, turn)
And there's this and that or some damn other thing…

But still
But still

And the river still flows wide,
And the gales of storms increase
The current's tumbling slide
Seaward, without cease.

Lines for my father

I think I owe some kind of explanation
As I grow tired and listless fingers writhe
Above the unpecked keyboard pad. I'm not
Quite out to blame you or your generation
For where I'm at tonight. You paid the tithe
That life exacts. It's sanctimonious rot
If we deny the pain of paying it—
And our denials never help one bit.

Unlike you, I found myself involved
In protest politics when I was young.
I spouted crap about the working class
While searching for a problem to be solved.
I mocked you then, since stirring tunes are sung
In brayed crescendos, with a blaze of brass
Booming triumphs won against the odds—
Unjust societies and jealous Gods.

You seemed so cautious—tastefully attired
With modest ties and polished wing-tipped shoes,
A cautious, kindly smile that reached your eyes.
A man to be respected, not admired,
Neither adulated nor abused.
Ambitions of an ordinary size
Were often past your reach. A nagging doubt
Set in, and now I know what that's about.

Tonight, I type these words as it gets late,
And no one calls to beckon me to bed.
I scoffed at what you'd craved—the tenure track,
The slow-accruing pension from the state,

The wife (who left you). Though you're good and dead
(And at this hour, my eyes are going slack)
And though you cannot answer, I'll report
—While having to imagine your retort—

That we're no happier than you, and can't
Quite seem to sit for tests that you had failed.
Our phones are packed with numbers we won't call.
The televisions blast a constant rant
That we ignore like letters still unmailed—
Or unconceived. Clichés about a ball
That's dropped don't work—or maybe don't apply.
We never picked it up. I wonder why.

This recognition's only dawning now
As streetlights speckle glimmers on your urn
Beside my unmade bed, and as I write
These words to you in lieu of sleep. Somehow,
The brays of drunks outside my window turn
Almost comforting, as if the night
Is full of us—insomniac, astray,
And muttering defiance at the day.

In humid summer weather

The spring had come, then gone, and I
Was up at night and lighting
Too many cigarettes—
Conjunctural Tourette's
Twisting each nocturnal cry.
The scene was unexciting,
The record all too clear.
I drank another beer,

And then I stared out past the leaves
That latticed every entrance
Along suburban streets
Where minor paracletes
Ascend at morning. Who believes
In sanctity and romance
When day will land too hard
Against the sun-bleached yard?

But her! With that ironic smile…
But her! With that retreating,
That glance across her back.
I think I should change tack
Or maybe rest a little while
Or watch the junk I'm eating…
But fuck it. What's the use?
I'll offer up a truce—

I'll stay on my side, she on hers.
I'll launch, at times, a sally,
A shock-and-awe of wit
(Remembering not to spit),
And she'll fire back, if she prefers
To even out the tally.

The contest might resume,
Unless… do I presume?

But will she ever think of me
—Or think of us together—
On hot and sleepless nights
When bare electric lights
Stretch out as far as you can see
In humid summer weather,
When I am far away
And out of things to say?

False alarm

"It's just a noise," you said as I woke up,
Cursing softly at the muffled yelling
Across the alley. "Just a noise," you said.
But had I heard a woman's voice—though faintly—
Call out, "Help!"? And though no sounds of struggle
Or shrieking sirens followed, I was taut,
Awake beside you, an edgy sentinel
Marking out perimeters with my hearing,
Plotting individual jurisdictions,
Spheres of influence, I guess—the point
At which the problem lay with someone else.
You looked at me and said, "Go back to sleep."

Still, I twisted the sheets around my toes,
Seething at the silence that revealed
No resolution, just a hint of plot—
A false alarm? Perhaps. The very quiet
Though, suggested dark hypotheses,
Unfalsifiable from where I lay.

As if by chance

When I looked at her, and when her lips
Pulled back to show her teeth, and when her voice
Broke into laughter, I could only think
Of moments that I'd pissed away, each choice
I'd left to others, and the careless slips
That landed me beside an empty drink.
That afternoon, I could have sworn I saw
A thinner, hopeful version of my face
Staring from behind her retinas—
Familiar, yes, the eyes, the skin, the jaw,
But in that instant somehow out of place.
It cast a knowing frown. The gravitas
Was overbearing. Nonetheless, we filled
The void with gossip, anecdotes and smut,
Comparing chatty journals—note by note.
Like poets, we dissembled in the rut
That each of us was in, our chances killed
By loss of nerve or failure to emote.
But still, a sneer could not have hurt me more
Than her clear laugh that sang of expectations
So long forgotten from a distant day
When youth still spread before me, and the poor
And pitiful attempts at explanations
Still lay in ambush, only years away.

Time zones

Of all the stupid things I could recall
Vaguely, at least, I happened to pick this:
A restaurant on Lindsey Street on Friday—
Smoky, crowded, tables none too tidy;
Above the packs of cigs, there was a hiss
Of muttered boasts, stage-whispered innuendoes,
And rambling anecdotes we'd heard before.
We knew quite well the cues for the crescendos,
For rises, drops, glissandos, and the trills
That ornamented stories of cheap thrills.

I was the thin one sitting by the window
Facing the Pizza Hut. At seventeen,
My hair was black; lips twisted in a smirk.
A pissed professor's son, a smart-assed jerk,
A bookworm almost trying to be mean,
I would hold forth on something that I'd read—
Or read about—and feeling very smart,
I'd talk some more. The crap I must have said
Would mortify me now (or so I'd think)—
I'll blame it on all the coffee that I'd drink.

And then there's Trevor, Lance… and what's-his-name—
The guy they busted with an ounce of pot
Stuck in his ass-crack coming from Mexico—
Jim or Jamie, something like that? No,
I can't remember. What the hell. It's not
Important, but I still can smell patchouli,
Recall the sleazy womanizing smile…
I hope I'm not upsetting you unduly.
My memory is not a total sty.
I'm not perverted, creepy, always high.

50

But still, those days are part of who I am,
Like my pollen allergy, the pack a day,
The drawl that sometimes ambles through my lips,
The bourbon that I drink at night in sips,
My passport, and the bills I have to pay.
With half-and-half, I learned to hold my own
And talk for hours on almost any subject—
Surrealism, Marx… or begging loans
To tip the waitress for another cup
Of coffee, hoping it would keep me up.

One night, Nathan (Surname…? Shit.) proclaimed
"External reality" to be subjective,
Freely quoting the Indian Spirit Father
Who'd waited for him in the acid blotter,
His rant subsided, and he turned introspective.
I burst out laughing—sober and unconvinced—
Which caused him to go cross-eyed for some reason
Before he gulped and blurted out, incensed,
That I could not remotely understand…
And might, perhaps, be working for the Man.

And though I didn't witness this, one day,
A regular came in, irate but ashen.
"Some kids were fucking in the parking lot."
I can't report that this occurred a lot;
The parents' bedroom was much more in fashion
Than screwing on asphalt out in public view
Chaperoned by cars and pick-up trucks—
Which was, of course, a stupid thing to do,
Cars moving in and out. No sense of style,
Those two. We talked about it for a while,

And guessed (though incorrectly) who it was.
But gossip soon resembles last week's paper,
Of little interest until history
Reclaims the headlines from obscurity.
Still, curiosity, till then, will taper
Off and dissipate. We all move on,
As will our lives and various new-found hobbies.
New things to hate or ways to get our groove on
Titillating, sweet—or even gory—
Wait in next week's human interest story.

It all adds up, you know, so many hours
Spent waiting in a place for things to happen.
But it was happening, and through the static
Of stoned pronouncements, grand and falsely vatic,
Through all the palaces we took a crap in,
We found each other, fuck-ups to a man—
Or woman. All that sentimental tripe
About "true friendship" wasn't quite the plan.
We fell in love, fell out, or went to college,
But there remained a thing that I'd acknowledge.

Now, not quite young but not yet old, I find
It's in the morning news and shitty weather
That most of us will find our close connections.
A stupid gaffe can lead to strong affections.
It's hardly fate that jumbles us together,
But having nowhere else to be. I know
It's "unpoetic," but I think I'm right:
There's something to the place you always go,
The booth that's yours, the same old conversation,
The boring, reassuring situation.

The restaurant I mentioned has new owners,
A different name, a different clientele.
I went last year and ordered a burrito
And found the difference somewhat bittersweet, though
Despite the past, I guess, it's just as well,
Since time accumulates in mounting strata,
Obscuring what came before with crushing weight,
Smashing artifacts, erasing data,
Leaving only fragments that might say
Who we were some given week or day.

II

Widen the angle, change the basic plot
From a comedy by Cheech and Chong
To something else—a tragedy? I doubt it,
But this is my life. There's no two ways about it,
Though not an action flick (it's far too long),
There's been a little bit of incident,
High drama, perhaps, the odd soliloquy,
The Rocky story (maybe just a hint—
I'm Ivy League, a hetero, and white;
"Against the odds" just doesn't sound quite right.)

But still, it's unexpected. How I swore
I wouldn't teach like Dad! I'd play guitar,
Write songs, and form a band to tour the globe.
Cool as crap and backlit with a strobe,
Cult following, too weird to be a star.
I'd rock your fucking world, man! Could've happened...

Well, maybe, maybe not. That was the dream.
It's not as if I wrote it off as crap and
Got a daytime job. The truth's more subtle—
I could have handled work at Pizza Shuttle,

With gigs on Fridays, practice on the weekend,
A rented room near the university
In my home town. I've known my share of squalor,
Anyway. Bohemian, white-collar,
In college for ten years—the Ph.D.
Reached me in my apartment in the Heights
(Washington that is), sweating through
A record heat wave, waking up most nights
To shouts in Spanish or sounds of breaking glass.
Welcome to the lumpen middle class.

But as I caught the train from the convocation,
Looking like Martin Luther in my hood
And robe and hat, the tail end of a phrase
Of music that I wrote in younger days—
D minor, heavy, slow, and fairly good—
Came back to me. I hadn't played the thing
(The song, not the guitar) in many years.
When I got home and played, the upper string,
Green with age, snapped off, and then the second.
I haven't replaced them since. No tunes have beckoned—

But was I stymied? Did I chicken out?
Or did I change, for better or for worse?
Was I seduced by serpents in the garden,

Or did I just accept I've got no part in
The pivotal scenes—unmentioned in the verse?
A cosmic extra on the ground in Babel,
I barely saw the tower scraping heaven.
"Give us Barabbas!" I'm shouting with the rabble,
And while the shepherds shuffle to the stable,
I'm on the couch next door and watching cable.

Uno momento, dude! We've all had dreams,
Mutually exclusive, and we choose.
Some friends of mine still play in bands today.
Some stayed in school like me. Some found their way
To squalid epiphanies in drugs and booze,
And some have children now. But then there's me,
Hither and yonder, shuttling through the time zones,
My rooms still rented, with an advanced degree
Not even framed yet, not quite one of those
Settled down into a place he "chose."

The trade-off's typical, the core dilemma
A classic one—in leaving one's hometown,
One's center's elsewhere. What's periphery
For those who stay to raise a family
Or whatthefuckever you do when settling down
Becomes the site of basic interaction
When prodigal through chance or conscious choice.
I'll be the last to sneer at the attraction.
Although I'm not a genius like Jimi Hendrix,
And just can't see myself tricked out in spandex,

Ambition still won't let me sleep sometimes.
Like an idiot howling for our notice,
A lovechild of the id and super-ego
That seems to follow us wherever we go,
Its schemes to thrust us forward and promote us
Are often mere reflex, heedless of direction,
Devoid of planning. Still, despite the gambits,
Stratagems, and lack of introspection,
The end result turns out to be regret
At not quite settling for what we can get.

What's not a gambit, though, if we're being honest?
The pipes might freeze. The car might be a lemon.
The children might turn criminal or whore.
The steady job might move to Bangalore.
A husband's eyes can stray to other women.
I could go on, but I think you get the drift.
We're betting on a game we can't quite play.
I wonder if the "safe move" gets short shrift,
But half expect it doesn't quite exist
In the poker face or a movement of the wrist.

But now I'm staring from my office window,
Listening to sounds in the corridor,
Voices I seem to recognize, that mingle
Into a sort of song, a tuneless jingle,
Percussive rain outside. I can't ignore
The symmetry of sound that still occurs
To me. Despite my swearing off ambitions
Of lasting fame, the subtle rhythm stirs
A hint of something larger than the rain
Behind my eardrum, racing through my brain.

III

From high school graduation to Ph.D.—
Staying in school consumed eleven years—
The butt-end of my youth—no piddling number.
I didn't piss the time away. Hell, slumber
Was always in short supply. Too many gears
Were creaking at once. The engine overheated
As I careened toward fictive finish lines,
A NASCAR approach to life: stay undefeated…
Accelerate, you bastard, hit the gas!
Take no prisoners, and kick some ass.

It wasn't a total wash, of course. I learned
To write to length. I lost my virginity,
Awkwardly, of course, but that's the way
It tends to go, still smoked a pack a day,
And I pronounced in all solemnity
That I was "on track," and when I reached the station,
I'd take a break—maybe for a night,
Or maybe longer. I dreamed of a vacation
Far away from everyone I knew
And all the garbage that I said I'd do.

A winter and a woman come to mind
From those days. Texas was slicked with ice.
She'd be in Oklahoma. Simple, right?
Leave in the afternoon, get in that night,
And watch for icy patches. Such advice
Ignores an aging Buick prone to stalling
When it got hot or cold outside. That day,

Although the prudent step involved me calling
Up to say I'd hold off on the journey—
And maybe working out power of attorney

In case of accident—I started driving…
And stalled out on an entrance ramp in Austin.
I slammed the thing in park and hollered, "Fucker!"
As just behind me, some speed-addled trucker
Honked furiously. I didn't care, being lost in
Memories of gray-green eyes. I fired
The engine up again, and it turned over.
The car shot forward. I was frantic, wired,
Surging with fear and lust and mounting speed,
Halfway between a snowball and tumbleweed,

Trying to reach her. Outside of Fort Worth,
I turned on the radio to Lynyrd Skynyrd—
A song I'd never really liked, a boozy
Boogie from a honky-tonk—a woozy
Shitkicker snarl and right hook to the innards—
Not my thing at all. But on that road,
The engine sputtering at eighty-five
While weaving past a convoy marked "wide load,"
I sang along to a glowing Forth Worth sky,
Even while thinking, "Shit, I'm going to die."

I cleared the Metroplex and shot past Denton,
Surged through Gainesville, and made it to the border,
Stopping off for gas in Marietta,
Then got back on the interstate to set a
Land-speed record (roughly), all in order

To reach the Norman exit and to meet her.
I did… although her flight had been delayed,
And all the punishment that my five-seater
Had taken was for nothing, but I'd exposed
The depths of my devotion. The evening closed

In the all-night restaurant that I've described—
To which I walked, leaving the car with Dad
To convalesce. The next day, she and I
Met up for drinks, and as the hours went by,
Convinced ourselves to fall in love. The mad
And brainless dash paid off; my course was set,
And by the time I climbed back in the Buick
And by the time she climbed aboard the jet
That took her to New York, we were together,
Undeterred by distance or the weather.

And when I headed down the interstate,
The storm had cleared. The engine was running better;
Problem surmounted, obstacles overcome
At twenty-two years of age! Yes, I succumbed
A bit to hubris, but then, each call, each letter,
And every e-mail I received would buoy me
Through the end of my undergraduate years—
Despite the catch that no one would employ me
In my field with just nothing but a BA
In history—and so I went away

To New York, to grad school, and to her,
And gradually, things started to run their course.
Dissertations, dreams of revolutions,
The rounds of demos, fragile constitutions—

As the years went by, I felt the force
Of gravity more keenly as I juggled
Too many balls—a grad-school activist,
With every quiet moment feeling smuggled,
Illicit, furtive, with piles of unwashed dishes
In the sink, with unacknowledged wishes.

It fell apart, of course. But still, tonight,
I'm sitting at home and writing this, about
A time when I took action, man, and beat
The urge to make an orderly retreat
And take a perverse comfort in my doubt.
Tactical victory, strategic blunder,
But still a win of sorts, I guess, although
The fact the whole endeavor buckled under
The crush of circumstance can't be ignored
(And though I'm hardly one to talk, she snored).

IV

Again, thoughts turn to home, my father dying,
The six months that I spent in my old bedroom
Surrounded by the remnants of a childhood
And adolescence I'd written off for good.
Or so I'd thought. There's only so much head-room
For new ideas, most of which revolve
Around the boring bits—like pension plans
And real estate. The old crap's not resolved
As much as reconfigured—our base condition
Is mainly altered through a life's attrition.

The cancer wore out Dad; it dug and carved
Through lesions on his legs and through his mind.
A vagueness settled in his eyes, his voice
Went slurry, and we had no choice
Except to watch him go—befuddled, blind,
And gradually losing his words. But still, the silence
Felt familiar, as if consoling talk
Would turn into a form of subtle violence,
A cop-out or a botched commiseration,
Another lie between the generations.

So many absences that year! I lost
A woman whom I thought I loved—and did,
I guess. And faced with a second looming crisis,
I fled for the first. To say I paid the price is
True, but only to a point. I hid
Behind my father's bed, as yet unable
To live a solitary life. At least
In dying, there's a thing that's oddly stable—
You know it's coming, and you can't pretend
That you were unaware how it would end.

And seeing it up close, as Dad grew weak,
As sentences, then words eluded him,
And as I changed his diaper when he pissed
And shat himself, his power to resist
The cancer weakening, only a dim
Sense of duty held me to my post.
Sometimes love is deeper than affection,
Even with those who care about you most.
I was there, and no alternative
Occurred to me but staying. We forgive

The dead more easily, since they can't make
Amends or clean the messes that they've made,
And I've found that the same goes for the dying,
Collapsing from within. There's no point trying
To hurt them from without. You feel betrayed,
Strangely, by the need to "let things go,"
To bear no grudges, leave the scores unsettled,
And all that other bullshit… But you know,
There's no scale to weigh the cons and pros;
It rusts and falls apart. The markets close.

But she was different, lovely and alive—
And living with another man, of course.
And she, a sudden stranger, seemed vivacious,
Laughing and distant. I'm hardly perspicacious
About these things, but it doesn't take much force
Of insight, really, to piece it all together.
She jumped the ship careening toward the ice-floes,
Read the charts and made note of the weather,
And headed for the lifeboat. I was sinking;
She rowed away, not facing me, unblinking.

Yeah, I fucked up, and she fucked up. That's all…
Although I went through every stupid gaffe
I made while weary, pissed off, or distracted
In a dark Socratic method, re-enacted
Every complacent shrug and careless laugh,
And went to shrinks. I swore off merely coping
Out of a sense of duty to a bed
Now mine alone. The futile, reflex hoping
For reconciliation, for exposure
Of 'all the shit she did to me', for "closure"

Evaporated in the end, though not
Through some celestial sunbeam, searing, bright—
I just got tired of all the arguments
I'd never make. Besides, the present tense
Almost compels a tone that's fairly light.
"Hey, man. I've got some beer and a DVD—
A Dario Argento flick with zombies.
Come on over. This shit you've gotta see!"
And that was healing, though I didn't think
That it would come through things I'd watch or drink.

But I got better. There was no single moment
When the clouds parted. It's more that they got thinner
And some of them blew away. I didn't see
Or analyze the meteorology.
It simply happened. Maybe it was a dinner
Or some dumb rerun that finally dissipated
The darkness—if not quite sunny, things got lighter.
An apathetic laugh, a hunger sated—
Hardly the stuff of history or song,
But misery should only last so long.

That's not to say that all has been forgotten.
The love affair is over; Dad is gone.
And though the former's faded, more or less,
Death's a bastard, and there's no redress,
No court for special pleading. "Just move on..."
Like hell I will! Don't talk to me about Jesus.
The ferry only carries you one way,
Whatever's on the other side to please us.
Our only maps are drawn from wishful thoughts,
And there's no bargaining or drawing lots.

V

Turn out the lights, double-check your bag,
And lock the office door. There goes the day.
It's mostly dark by now. A distant bell
From an unknown church is clanging against the swell
Of honking traffic stalled out on the way
To homes out in the suburbs. But not yet.
You're pausing in the hall and hesitating.
The weather murmurs, menacing and wet,
In rain that taps on a nearby office window.
You almost look as if you might stay in, though

You really need to leave. You smile a moment—
It's just a smile, not sultry or seductive.
Your slender fingers resting on the key
Twist into motion. Almost offhandedly,
You nod in my direction, and I give
A quick nod back. This moment that we share,
A chance encounter on two different paths
That merged together for a while, is rare
Enough, of course, as is the sudden thought
That this is what there is. We'd better not

Dismiss it, since the company's not bad,
The anecdotes are funny, and the journey
Is long enough as is. Goodbye for now.
See you tomorrow—or sometime, anyhow,
Suited for work or babbling on a gurney,
A weekend (or perhaps a decade) older,
A little worse for wear—or maybe radiant.

This moment may burn out—or it may smolder
Underneath a season's pile of leaves.
Too soon to say. One knows what one believes—

But it's a hunch, an educated guess
Like turns one makes wandering through a city
One barely knows and navigates on impulse—
A half-remembered grid and ancient temples
Anchoring your direction sense through gritty
Cul-de-sacs and teeming, dead-end streets.
Global positioning and mobile phones
Can't sort it out—we're here. The high-tech cheats
Merely confirm it in pixilated maps
That point to pots of gold, leaving out the traps.

You know the traps—the crap we have to say
About "careers," the fear of dying lonely
And far away from a decent cup of coffee,
The purred, "That was fantastic... now get off me"
The looking back and muttering "If only...,"
The times you didn't drink... or drank too much,
The times you settled, growing slightly bored,
Half a decade gone—"We'll keep in touch."
Or maybe not. Traps come in many sizes,
Bristling with pensions, salaries, and prizes.

But for a moment, it seems a convenient fiction—
The stuff we have to say so we'll get hired,
The conferences, CVs, and articles,
The credits here and there, the particles
We jam into portfolios. I'm tired—

And so are you, I think—but still we spend
Our evenings in, take up new assignments,
Work our asses off, and wonder when
The pace will slow—or will we acclimate?
Until we do, I guess I'll stay up late

On week nights, and I'll make a pot of tea,
Arrange the books, and do a bit more writing
In my two-room flat, avoiding bed,
All for a harebrained scheme to "stay ahead,"
Bashing out paragraphs in shitty lighting…
But that's for later. Now, we're closing down,
Heading into the cold and teeming dusk—
Before we dash to opposite sides of town,
Always in transit, moving from afternoon
And into night, which always ends too soon.

I had a dream last night, and there you were
With me and all the people that I've mentioned,
Sitting around a table in a diner.
I don't recall much else, though it's a minor
Point in the end. The invite's well-intentioned,
Impossible, of course, since as I've noted,
The place is now a Mexican restaurant
And wasn't quite your style back then, but floated
In clouds of hormones, tobacco, and cannabis—
All of which comes down to saying this:

Afternoon-special exhortations, all
That *carpe diem* shit they spout at kids…
There is a point, but it isn't what they think.
It's not a pretty house and high-paid shrink
And staying off the pipe and off the skids
That we should chase, but this, a crystallized
Moment or so, when you're looking past the hallway,
And something glimmers deep in your pale eyes.
I don't know what it is, and wouldn't ask.
Besides, it's getting late. The daily tasks

Are done, for now at least, so go on home.
The papers don't move at night and will remain
At their posts like watchmen, half asleep,
To blink and yawn at morning. What doesn't keep
Is this: the lingering imprint of a stain
Of coffee on a sleeve, spilled late at night,
The perfect joke (although you had to be there),
The way your neck was bending to the right
As you smiled primly, nodded, and walked away
Into the daylight's ultimate decay.

William Montgomery's Guide to New York City
(2008)

New York is appalling, fantastically charmless and elaborately dire.
                                        —Henry James

I: Inwood

Thin-skinned in cold—William's extra sweater
Only held out the first wave of assault.
His scarf was soaked, trousers slightly better.
It's just the time of year, and no one's fault.

No one's fault? When nobody demanded
That he remain holed up in an uptown flat
Midwinter, voluntarily remanded
To life with a sofa and a cranky cat
Who'd watched him warily as he got dressed,
Slacks and a tie, expensive overcoat—
Quite debonair. The cat was unimpressed,
Turning to puke a fur ball from its throat.

Marooned upon this island in December,
Face as anonymous as everyone
Who passed him with no reason to remember
Who he was. The day had just begun,
But bled into the others, like the crowd
That passed before his aching, blinking eyes,
Paces straight and quick, snarled catcalls loud—
Pure incident, devoid of all surprise.

Columbia degrees, a teaching job,
Inherited money seeping from the bank
Like melting snow. Half dandy and half slob,
Underslept but restless. You can thank
The cups of bodega coffee he consumed
While rushing to the subway for his state—

Or note it as symptomatic and subsume
It into a life of always running late.

Did Henry James's lip curl in the same
Dismissive way when he returned to visit
So many years ago? But William's game
Is played by different rules. *Oh, really, is it?*

II: Harlem

Things get recycled—see that storefront there?
That's where Marcus Garvey used to labor
For his dreams of Africa, that place where hair
Gets cut and styled. Not quite its neighbor,
But down the street—see that restaurant?
Yeah, the IHOP. That's where Malcolm X
Worked in its dancehall days, a favored haunt
For music, speed, hard booze, and no-frills sex
Before he turned to Allah.

                 That's where the *Crisis*
Was—right there. All gone and hardly noted,
Except for place names, references to "Isis,
The African Queen of Beauty."

                   But the bloated
Downtown belly extends beyond its belt,
The cordon at the top of Central Park.
The old divisions hold, but seem to melt
Around the edges. Politicos remark
About the "progress" the neighborhood is making,
But Claude McKay's turned out by Colonel Sanders.
A different hunger needs a different slaking.

Or perhaps the gorging calls for different slanders.
We've heard it all, about "community"
And its imperatives, about "the people,"
About the things at stake when what will be
Isn't what we want.

A church's steeple
Rises from the brownstones, and a choir
Sings a spiritual that longs for freedom
For everyone beneath that modest spire,
While asking, all the same, that God redeem them.
Jazz Age licentiousness is not their lot.
The Cotton Club is hardly what it was
(And under different management). The hot
Rhythms of yesteryear have cooled. "The Cause"
Isn't what it used to be, although
A beggar on Lenox shuffles through a blast
Of frigid air, mingled with light snow.
The Jordan's still ahead.

"We're free at last!"
No, not free yet; a mumble for some change
Whips past William's ear as he descends
To catch the A, foreign and estranged.
He gives a quarter, as if to make amends.

III: Battery Park

Sucking up the end of a cigarette
And huddling up against a tingling rail,
Kinetic with winter, his dark eyes wet
With either rain or tears, he saw the pale
Gray of winter sky against the shore
That framed the churning water in the bay.
The ferry pulled away, then turned once more.
It's back and forth. You cannot get away,
With Ellis Island hovering to your right,
A closed-up shop, and nearer, that green statue
With torch held high against incipient night
Seems to provide a light by which to catch you.

It's just impression. William's line predates
The stinking masses who came in that way
To tenements in these United States.
Johnny-come-latelies in a different day,
Whose Anglophone descendents crowd the places
Their ancestors abandoned for New Jersey,
Long Island, Westchester County. Now, their faces
Look out of place like William's, hardly worthy
Of their addresses in rough neighborhoods
Still bitter with the lingering aftertaste
Of poverty and crime and "damaged goods"
Walking the streets.

                    But still, we shouldn't waste
The remnants of the hint of sun behind
Predictable walls of cloud before the dark
Turns deeper and colder, angry and unkind.

The dusk is settling in the city park.
And William makes his way to catch his train
Uptown in the half-light of the IRT
As unseen skies release a sheen of rain
Onto the crowded sidewalks, fitfully.

IV: The East Village

Teeming as always with the student crowd
Spilling out of dive bars, overpriced,
But otherwise the same, each jukebox loud
And every conversation still enticed
By background noise and booze into a shout,
The streets pulse with domesticated menace,
All in good fun, of course, an evening out,
Playing at bohemia.

                Within us,
There remains an urge to "push our luck,"
To play at Ginsberg or Warhol, though we're not
Tormented artists anymore. We're stuck
With simulacra, battles already fought
And mostly lost to money and the trend
To bulldoze stinking squats and hire more cops
With cries of "urban renewal." In the end,
We're left with brighter lights and finer shops.

But hail the old embattled clubs and centers
Of those without some other place to go!
All praise the icons and the fictive mentors
Of scenes that, nowadays, they'd hardly know!

The slammers still line up at the Nuyorican;
The rock bands still jam out in basement rooms.
William's still shitfaced on a frigid weekend
In bars sealed up as snug as antique tombs.

V: Greenwich Village

Stagger west, and past Fifth Avenue,
The streets seem wider, the rents a little steeper.
Turn south a ways, make towards NYU,
All the while, working a little deeper
Past the factory where women flung
Themselves from upper-storey windows when
Trapped by fire—a tragedy well-sung,
One for the history books. But that was then.

Working-class, bohemian—then what?
An enclave full of WASPs, Italians, blacks,
Poe, Millay, and Cummings, though they're not
Around here anymore, or coming back.

Washington Square. Townhouses to the north
With narrow top-floor windows where the maids
Once slept. Go west, the gay guys sally forth
From bars that, once, the vice squad used to raid.
Jazz bars, record stores; the straight and bent
Merge along the streets, although, they're now
Exiled elsewhere due to higher rent.

Despite our dark attempts to disavow
The newfound cleanliness, a sense remains
That things still happen here, where Joan Baez
Once sang in the park. In spite of all the strains
And all the yuppies in the new cafes,
We're meant to be here.

          An old cacophony
Still races through the conversations, blended
Warp and woof, into a tapestry,
Frayed at the edges, unlikely to be mended,

But *us,* despite it all. And William lurches
Past the bars, the clubs, the dizzy blend
Of noises echoing from grey stone churches
To catch his train and bring it to an end.

VI: Morningside Heights

Broadway, 116th; a wrought-iron gate.
Security guards and Goddesses protect
The university, their easy state
Of vigilance is not so much respect
For what they guard so much as a disdain
For what's outside the square within. Look through
The gates to College Walk washed slick with rain
Where leftists hawk the *Socialist Review*
To students who ignore them.

          So it was
And is and always will be, till the time
As we evolve through paths professors trace
From boiling seas to rank primordial slime
To what we are and past.

          But can we face
The end of this—the Butler Reading Room,
Byzantine grandeur in every hall and dome?
And would it be its renaissance or doom
If these gates truly opened?

          Far from home,
The would-be scholars cling to student lounges
And faraway apartments and a check
That pays the rent, and everybody scrounges
Just to get by, and everyone's a wreck.

But Alma Mater's on her metal perch,
Dispassionate as we're supposed to be,
Stern as a preacher in an old-time church,
And trying to convey the mystery

Of Ivy-League… erudition? Arrogance
More like it, an aristocratic swagger
Made, not born, quick to take offence,
Well-spoken, though the sleeve contains a dagger.

And William's one of them, he cannot alter
His path this late, almost foreordained,
Although his gaze can slip askance and falter,
Although the vista's bleak, at present strained
Through rain and grandeur.

                Still he passes by
The statues like he's done before for years—
Besides, we're all expected to ask why,
To search for meaning, submerging reflex fears
In the search for truth. He heads straight for the stacks,
The shelf that's almost his on the second floor,
And he sits down, a brick wall to his back,
And isn't so uneasy anymore.

VII: Central Park

Bethesda Garden's past the promenade,
And couples walk, arm and arm, meander through
The famous scenery, bucolic, staid,
Though framed at the edges by a distant view
Of penthouse roofs, but in between, the trees,
Leafless in winter, hint we can abscond.
The water ripples as a frigid breeze
Sweeps past the fountain, whips around the pond
And makes for Harlem. But we're *here* for now.
This isn't ersatz space, but time. The shape
Of the winding paths, Caulfield's carousel,
The way the buildings on the water ape
A place we wish existed once, the swell
Of distant voices that don't quite sound like ours—
Too genteel somehow to quite be us,
A withered generation.

                Car horns sour
The reverie. A cross-town city bus,
Laden with commuters makes its rush
Through ditch-like roads somewhere beyond our sight.
It's mostly far away; a reverent hush
Descends, but somehow doesn't sound quite right.

Break's over, I'm afraid. No time to linger
In some besotted, chilly reverie.
Try to hail a cab and give the finger
As it surges with the traffic frantically.

VIII: Fort Greene, Brooklyn

Off the tourists maps, but on the G Line,
Faded genteel and newly gentrifying
Wide avenues where traffic makes a beeline
To… where? There isn't any use denying
That William only worked out here, his phone
Is in a different area code, adjacent
To be sure. Manhattanite, alone,
The outer boroughs seemed a bit complacent,
Not quite the place he lived. Did marriages
Last longer here, or was it an illusion
Created by the baby carriages
Flowing through the park. The shrill confusion,
If not quite mute, is quieter out here,
The buildings rise, but reach a little lower.
A city of churches still. The spires still rear
Above the brownstones. Somehow, we move slower
In their presence till we reach the stop
(The *Times* in hand, half-read), Manhattan-bound
To stare at where we live, then quickly drop
Our eyes to the caterwauling on the ground.

IX: Inwood (Reprise)

Good night, dear city, as the radiator
Clicks its lullaby, and as the cat
Purrs in harmony, then slightly later
Moves to the next room, and that is that,
At least for now. William's stereo
Weaves just above them with familiar songs—
Clearly enough, although the volume's low,
And in that moment everything belongs:

The shadows playing on the stucco ceiling,
Books stacked on a narrow window sill,
An incongruous, almost peaceful feeling,
And as he fades to dreams, a subtle thrill

At being where he is despite the rent,
The maddening imperatives of day,
Too much to drink, and too much money spent
On far too little. Still, it drifts away

Like women that you see on trains, their beauty
Stunning amidst the squalor that surrounds
Their reveries. Stern-eyed cops on duty,
Pistols at their sides, walk through their rounds.

Good night, you beauties, faces stuck in books
Or haughtily dismissing every man
Who meets your eyes with sharp and scornful looks.
You can't escape our dreams and cannot plan
Where they will lead.

                    Good night, my dearest friends,
Although the days are busy, and we rarely
See each other. Still we'll make amends

And get together soon, if only barely
In some old bar or in a city park
To make up legends. It's far too large for us,
And renders us epic as the day turns dark
And as you run to try to reach the bus.

The music ended; the cat had gone away,
And modest shadows on the ceiling leapt
To fill the gaps of light. Another day
Was over. William closed his eyes and slept.

from *Obscure Classics of English Progressive Rock* (2012)

Ice Storm

Isn't it beautiful, the way the ice
holds the streets in stasis, but with glints
that flash their warnings as cautious tires roll
between the patches? You and I both wince,
consider going out, but then think twice.
Cars skid; arms break. The season takes its toll.

We're looking out from in, or there from here,
a slight or great removal from the source
of each refracted image of the chill.
I'm over here; you're over there, of course,
and if the air is frigid, it is clear
as night goes on, glittering and still.

Apartments

No ghosts as yet, but just a hint of fever
(the fan's still in its box) and foreign noise.
A virgin phone squats on its new receiver.
Undusty window sills are bare but ready
for clocks, for brown, anemic plants, their poise
temporary, fragile and unsteady.

There have been other places, across the river,
or oceans, time zones—other furniture,
with curtains cutting light to just a sliver,
those old apartments populated still
with women whom you recollect as "her."
They haven't called; you doubt they ever will.

Each lease becomes an act of...not forgetting,
but somehow letting go. Old places live
with different faces in a familiar setting:
lives you'll never know, but comprehend,
scenes of errors not yours to forgive,
broken hearts no longer yours to mend.

Out of shot

Outside the window, different shades of light
imply the movements of other lives. A car
screeches into action in the lot.
The rails on the beds, the IV drips,
and light blue gowns sequester us from *them,*
dressed in their daytime civvies, late for work,
fumbling with car keys—we can't hear the jingle
or muttered curses at cacophonous
alarm clocks on the bed stands we can't see.

We see a bit, of course, from where we are
and know what's going on beyond our sight.
The window, pigeon dropping-smeared, lets in
a limited tableau, a TV screen
without commercial interruption, cast
with nothing but extras, a wide, extended shot
without a zoom to close-up—since the star
of the series is convalescing off the screen
and watching from a bed that's not his own.

Fragment from an American folk song,
circa.2003

You're drunk and you're bored and you're slouching beneath
an unwatched TV while that twat Toby Keith
sings on the jukebox. It beggars belief,
but Saddam's "at the top of his list."

It goes on like this until late in the night.
You can say what you think, but it might mean a fight,
so you fondle your beer with your mouth closed up tight,
but your free hand closed up in a fist.

A change of season

A sunny girl from Northern climes,
hair and skin both honey-bright
with wide blue eyes, and in the gray
of an early spring, exuding light,

she reeks of health. Her diary
is crammed with fitness, every date
a rushed itinerary, full
of things to keep her in that state—

aerobics and organic fruit
—rip the flesh and suck the pips!—
bike to work from a D4 home…
until one day, her bright gaze slips

and falls on him, Italianate—
subtle, with a hint of threat,
bling on his finger. And his voice
cloys with a charm that makes her wet.

So he's "in business"—various things—
the sort of wealth with wads of cash
from nowhere in particular,
a sleek Mercedes, and a stash

of blow from South America
back at his place (with potpourri
above the toilet, and the sink
crowned with mousses from Italy).

Fast-forward through frenetic nights,
romantic dinners, snorted coke,
flowers delivered to her work,
their favorite song, their private joke.

He takes the gambit, and succeeds.
A ring's produced, and she says yes
on a long walk through Phoenix Park.
The wind is blowing from the west,

wafting and dulcet, as the sun
sinks down behind the stands of trees,
promising in a breathless rush
a life of indolence and ease.

But still, they pack and make their way
to meet the "Family," now hers,
with bodyguards and smoking wives
with Gucci bags and hideous furs.

Proserpina looks up and gasps,
stupid in her shock, her scream
unuttered as they pull her down,
beyond the reeking, corpse-choked stream

burbling with the failing pleas
that echo through the dark and wet,
rushing into darker caves
beyond forgiveness or regret.

Minor character

The bit-part actor takes a hurried drag,
stubs the cigarette with a velvet shoe,
and makes his entrance from stage left to say,
"Clubs, bills, and partisans! strike! beat them down!
Down with the Capulets! down with the Montagues!"
First Citizen's speech is over. Exeunt.
The scene's been set. The actor heads backstage
then has a whiskey in the bar next door.

Four acts to go on stage. We know the plot,
the balcony, the swooning, the belated
realization the Citizen was right—
although he's gone and long since out of costume,
faded into anonymity,
the greater, uncommemorated suffering.

Heuston Station

But as the train pulled out, the sun was shining,
though cautiously—a woman's guarded smile
at some weak play of humor. Silver lining?
No. Perhaps a respite for a while
in a land of drizzle and too many queues,
resentful songs of rebels long since beaten,
an awful shrink-wrapped sandwich still uneaten,
and evenings killed off with too much booze.

Art house cinema

Opening Credits

Accordion music's joined by clarinet
and then the director's name, a cityscape,
a human form, still just a silhouette.
A shot. The shadow's down. A quick escape
as the well-known actor's name bursts through the gloom,
followed by the girl's, though in this room,
we know the plot already, from a class
or book or film review, what to expect
from the director's work—a weekend pass,
a retrospective, and a familiar name,
a shibboleth of awe, at least respect
or reverence, the reason that we came.

Think clichés—how opposites attract,
how he met her, or how the fight was won,
the underdogs who carry the second act
with dignity—although it's in good fun.
But here, tonight, it's slightly more abstract
in black and white. And this is how we like it—
take the convention, batter it, and strike it
with something else. The opening scene's begun

on a European street
all age and shadows, early summer heat
implied by the heroine
in a svelte new sun dress, delicate and thin
as a modish cigarette
(the actress will get cancer, but not yet),
and the hero of the caper
sips coffee as he burrows through the paper
at a picturesque café—

ironic calm, since trouble's on the way.
The actor speaks his line—
subtitled, yes, but we all think that's fine
despite the bad translation
and revel in the iconic situation

and settle further in our seats to see
what lies in store for them, and you, and me.

Entr'acte

The griminess of plot and seedy bars
that dot the film like tumors as our hero
chain-smokes through misfortune, dodging cars
in search of a fortune—or reprieve?—drops out,
and as we go from racing speed to zero,
we stop for a moment near a waterfront.

The key's to always *get* it, not to pause
or linger on ideas till the end,
but focus on procedure—the swift caress
of tracking shots, the way the lights portend
significance, the slight off-kilter clause
in a sentence. It's all in the technique—
fifty years ago or just last week,
her face has stayed that oval of remorse,
her line that classic of the femme fatale
(though only understood as text, of course,
in yellow script). This is what we seek
in shadows-and-caves suggestions of celluloid:
a moving, pure alignment of it all.

Extras in the background play at cards.
The city's emptiness becomes a void
beyond established landmarks. Her and him.
Or maybe not, although they're at the center
of the shot, an alternate dimension
between the exposition of the plot
and some conclusion that will skirt convention.
But still we linger. This is the money shot,
the poster on a wall, the cultured hard-on,
the pregnant moment that the lovers part on
to be reunited only near the end
in farcical mischance that hardly matters.
Despite the car chase and the final splatter,
this is the *mise en scène* that will transcend
the train ride home, the vagaries of style.
We won't forget his shout, her rueful smile.

Closing Credits

Darkness, always darkness, at the start,
and silence till the closing credits roll.
Each one of us retreats into ourselves,
an act of solipsism for the art
of reverential silence, of control
of feelings that we cannot call our own.

Our passions stay uncooled
within our bundled clothes, and all are fooled
by silent soliloquies
that argue with the images one sees
onscreen or in the slush
of a February night. The sluggish rush

101

to reach the train slows down.
Is that something glowing in the brown
of a melting pile of snow?
What's *that* doing here? We don't quite know—
a cast-off cigarette
lies in a drift, smoldering and wet.
And then we walk away
to a city street, a different shade of gray,
and a static traffic jam,
and you're still you, and I'm still what I am.

Jimmy Carter, King of America

I must have been—what?—four when Jimmy Carter
stepped out of Air Force One on the TV set,
smiling and shaking hands despite the polls
and all the shit that must've been going down.
There were exorcisms in Tehran,
with "Death to the Great Satan!" on the lips
of mullahs, while the Soviet helicopters
swarmed Afghanistan. But I was four
and didn't know quite who the hell it was
waving at us, so I asked my mom.

"That's Jimmy Carter, Quincy." But who's he?
"The leader of our country." Oh, our *king*.
I'd heard the fairy tales and thought I knew
the ins and outs of war and politics.
But he didn't look that regal in a suit
like something that my dad would wear to church.
No crown or scepter—and what was with the surname?
Kings had numbers, or really awesome titles
like "Lionheart," "the Mad," "the Third," "the Bold,"
"the Great"—or even "the Magnificent."

I went outside and played catch with my dad,
who laughed when I explained what I had learned
about our king. But grown-ups always laughed
(or so it seemed) at my discoveries—
that the sky was far too high to reach,
even for them, that toilet water swirled
the same direction every time you flushed,
that snow was frozen rain. I let him laugh,
and then my Dad and I went in to eat
the supper that was always on the table.

King Carter was replaced by Ronald Reagan—
who had a different last name, and was older.
I learned about elections, the tradition
of voting on a Tuesday for our leaders—
all citizens "like us." But soon enough,
I heard of Contras out in jungles, islands
swarming with Marines… and slavery,
homeless people, and laid-off auto workers,
and that our TV came from far away,
a place whose name I couldn't quite pronounce.

You can't go back, of course. The TV set
is in some dump in central Oklahoma.
A different generation's in the yard
of the house my mother sold when she dumped Dad.
I've also learned that you don't need a king
to have an empire, court, and sycophants
while the poor get screwed, and every day, the news
comes like a tedious joke, in sober suits,
straight-faced insanity that we switch off,
then heat a frozen dinner from the fridge.

We all have our needs

I watch two twentysomethings on the train
and know what's on their minds, their faces stuck
in cautious non-expression as their brains
grow giddy with their unexpected luck.
But why suppress their feelings? There's no shame
in wanting it, in getting some at last,
a little closer with each station passed—
a gonad's urge that no one needs to name.

But when you score, something always slips
from balled-up sheets, from minds, from frenzied lips.
And past the press of chests and groins and hair
a silence settles—trumping everything
that you can say, or hold to, even cling
against yourself—and saturates the air.

If God is good

If God is good, and if the weather holds,
and if the horse comes in, we might allow
a glint of teeth between a face's folds—
a smile that promises, at least for now,
that God is good, and that the weather holds.

If life is chance, if chaos is our lot,
and if the math can't quite be reconciled
—even with itself—then what we've got
is probability. But dice fly wild,
since life is chance, and chaos is our lot.

If she were near, and I could hear the sound
of placid breathing up against my ear,
her reassuring sleep might bring to ground
the migratory urge that brought me here
if she were near, if I could hear the sound.

If God were good, and if the sky stayed blue,
and she were here, and all the numbers fit,
and all the things that I believe were true,
would I notice, even for a bit,
that God is good, and that the sky stays blue?

The leap

*If I am capable of grasping God objectively, I do not believe, but
precisely because I cannot do this I must believe.*
                                                —Soren Kierkegaard

It's not the fall that acrophobics fear,
the fatal inattention, as the body
accelerates, and distant crawling figures
whirring on the ground gain features, voice,
reflex cacophonies of screams and honking
as the concrete of the street approaches.

They fear the jump itself, the narrow ledge
bordering a moist and chilly sky,
the moment when a day like any other
picks up speed and plunges into space
that's always there, in lungs and hair and eyes,
but only now regarded for itself,

beyond immense, its endless grandeur felt
despite its invisibility, the shape
of fronts that spread across the continent
in forms that only metaphor reveals
in lines and arrows on a map. Out there,
the sky is palpable; the gusts are strong.

The realization gives but little comfort
until, despite the snap of wind, they sense
their feet against the ground again, the air
the merest pockets in the curving arches
between the toes that dig into their socks
and heels that swivel, testing what's below.

107

Sceneshifts

I

Just past the Georgian buildings, as I near
the traffic-choked bridge, I listen to the noises
that burble like bubbles rising from the river,
stagnant and stinking. Not exactly feared,
those unwashed memories, although I shiver—
and blame the cold. The sounds of far-off voices,
slightly familiar, whisper parts of phrases
that I should recognize, as unseen gazes
rake my hair—or is that just the wind?
Why do I think of you, and do I stutter
as I cross the bridge and reach its end,
breath uneven, pulse a nervous flutter?

City of absences! I tried to hold
the memory like fading rays of sun
that glisten in puddles, shifting to reflections
of headlights as the sun sets. It gets cold.
Disoriented by random interjections,
I speed up till I'm nearly at a run
and almost home in streets devoid of you,
with strangers passing and a constricted view
of steeples and a river and the stars
suffusing through city lights to reach the ground,
offset by the sound of soft guitars
filling my head with wistful wisps of sound.

Lay me down to sleep, if I can rest,
O Lady of My Memory and spread
the sheets above me, covering my face,
until the heartbeat throbbing in my chest
diminishes, and flows of dreams erase

my thoughts. Unsure if I'm asleep or dead,
and heedless of the consequences, I
will stay here, motionless, beneath a sky
both starless and unseen, a canopy
of stucco framing this, my mute repose,
and you, O Lady of My Memory,
will lie beside me as my eyelids close.

II

A shift of scene. Move forward from one stop
onto another as it's getting brighter.
The bus pulls in, and I almost drop
my cigarette while fumbling with my lighter.

"Were you the man who used to sing the songs
out on the square
for change or bags of weed
as passers-by would pause to yell requests
in other native languages—
love songs, dance songs, the news of the day?"

And silence
as memories returned that weren't mine
but anecdotes of someone else's travel,
thumb to the road, a foreign subway line,

a threadbare coat just starting to unravel.
"Jhoo are Eenglish yes?" The look goes blank.
"You've got the wrong guy." Pause. "Oh, you're the *Yank.*"

Which one are you? Which woman's absent shoulder
won't support my head as I wake up wincing
and stare out the window, ever so slightly older,
memories more jumbled and unconvincing?

But the practicalities…
Did I remember to pay the parking meter,
keep my vowels up front, pronounce my R's,
lock the door, shut off the stove and heater,
and cast my lot against the distant stars,
savoring the morning's cautious glow,
overdressed for as-yet-distant snow?

And a series of busses
and tourists chatting in my native tongue,
and I thought, *Dear God, have I been gone so long?*
as I shared in the distaste
for the ignorance of the timetables
and the denominations of the local currency,

and I stared
at the expanses of new estates
miles away from the anecdotes
of aging buskers.

The memories are running far away,
a squeal of tape rewinding, back to shops
stocked full of sweets, the sky a bluish gray
above an empty rugby pitch, then stops,

and for the merest fraction of a second,
a half of an iota of an instant,
I can feel her head against my shoulder,
remember fondling locks of curly hair…
and know that this is much too much to bear.

Did we break even?
Did we make out like bandits?
No, more like clumsy, eager adolescents
groping in cars, a quick ejaculation,
and crises on the family vacation.

We wondered if we still could make it back
on what was in the tank, and held on tight,
a love of necessity, a shocking lack
of exit plans within the incipient night.

And in the press of half-formed recollections,
tickets in pockets, and noisy interjections
from passengers debating their directions,
the scene shifts further as a brooding dawn
glowers above the trees, and we move on.

III

Rain. And the river, wrathful, surges
unheeded in the headiness of a half-dream night.
The living lurch in layers of the skull,
and I rise retching, wracked with the sense
of a meeting missed, a marred assignation.
Is fever at fault? The foul weather
whips past the walls, but the wind mutters,

O Muse of Memory, mother of the restless,
who delves in dreams, digging for samples
in stab-marks of stars or the stutters of phrases
I couldn't quite acquire for my tongue.

And you, who lie asleep beside the water,
alone, in company, dead drunk or sober.
riding high, incipiently hungover,
someone's lover, someone else's daughter—
guarding the gold that rests in the riverbed
even if its gleam is false. Unseen,
it can't be turned to numbers, but instead
can only shine.
                    I don't know where it's been,
what bold adventurers have sallied forth
from Hyperborean strongholds in the North
to seize it, or what gouty Nibelung
whispered nothings through his half-held breath
(not much to look at, surely, but well-hung).
But each scenario's been done to death.

Watch over me, maiden, as I drift to sleep,
and sing your arias in gentler keys,
voices like a river, flowing deep.
Alto clef, not brazen Valkyries.

IV

But here, a dashed-off note, and here, the wreck
that rises to the surface for a second,
propelled into view by violent turbulence
I cannot see. The remnants of the deck
rise at an angle.
                    But no mermaids beckoned;
someone else's filched inheritance
came to nothing. I watched from far away
as if the mess were none of my concern,
as if it were footage filmed some other day.
Type it up, then save and press Return.

Old e-mails on the screen,
and sentences no longer meant return
in pallid cyberlight, the time between
shrunk to an instant; embers start to burn.

And I must have reread those words
at least a hundred times

as the rain fell in bitch-slaps on the roof
and the frozen pizza turned brown in the oven with the temperature
        set too high,
and two drunks on the street staggered by singing "The Fields of
        Athenry"
as they stuffed their faces with lukewarm chips,
and a teenaged girl, young and beautiful and aching with the fatal
        joy of being human,
pressed her middle finger to the window of the Subway shop.

Forget her
        and do better.
                        I'd forgotten
everything, except for random jetsam
that mingled in the surf, bleached out and rotten,
items that haunt you… *only if you let them.*
But I remembered, far too well, a place
no longer mine, a different port of call,
and botched itineraries, and a face
that launched some ships.
                        It wasn't that way at all.

                        V

Midnight; dull electric bulbs resume
their vigil over stacks of crumpled paper,
dirty dishes, an ashtray's unkempt bloom…
and memories of the way her fingers taper...

114

That weekend night, the music blared, its bass line thick.
I took a corner spot,
watched nubile rear-ends shaking to a Latin beat,
and ordered up a shot
then got another beer that cost me far too much.
I didn't dance at all.
I wondered if I still looked suave—or still looked thin
while sitting by the wall.
Those evenings end. They rarely go the way you'd like.
The morning doesn't care
about the disks the hipster deejay spun that night
or whether you were there.
They just let go when weekdays are too much to stand.
They buy another round
and lose themselves in dance and endless draughts of beer
and gushing throbs of sound.
Why can't they goddamn see the well-lit exit sign,
the reasons to mistrust
the dead end of the sensual, the awkward blink
that frames that gaze of lust?

Paracetamol. A drink of water.
A bad kebab, a wince through one last smoke.
The heat's set where it was, though it seems hotter.
I don't know why, but it's the perfect joke…

I didn't see the city much that languid week.
I barely went outside,
her head by mine, a single, narrow pillow shared,
the gratitude and pride
that she was sleeping next to me… it still seems strange,

115

like someone else's life,
or maybe like a thin and arid fantasy
of someone else's wife.

It's just another round you never mean
to drink, and then you find yourself outdoors,
dew on the ground—a slick and chilly sheen—
then street, then locks, familiar corridors…

Now no one's hands but mine will rearrange the sheets
in night-time tugs of war.
There's no one here to grumble at my coarser ways
or grimace at my snore,
and in the short term, I will lie awake in bed
and murmur to my pride
that this is just another stage of life, and that
I'm glad she left my side.

And heedless of the consequences, I
will stay here, motionless, beneath a sky
both starless and unseen, a canopy
of stucco framing this, my mute repose,
and you, O Lady of My Memory,
will lie beside me as my eyelids close.

No snow yet in Galway

There's no snow yet in Galway, only mist.
"Celtic" or not, it clings to everything
like fever sweat, and even here, indoors,
swaddled in blankets, giddy from caffeine
in endless cups of tea, the damp persists.
The Corrib flows, dirt brown, into the sea.

But cut to distant relatives and news
of ice in North America, power lines
that icicles have snapped like rubber bands.
Forecasts of rain. I'm here. Another year
of watching tickers on the TV screen,
sick and groggy, coughing through the night

as others weigh the risks of being where
they're loved for no good reason, for their blood
or for their childhoods. Even if it hurts
(it always hurts somehow), the recognition
of something festering can reassure
them that they're *them* despite the distances.

No snow in Oklahoma, only ice,
covering driveways, stranding pizza guys
on half-deserted entrance ramps, while lights
flicker on and off. The e-mail brings
a blustery reproach. *You coming home?*
Thanks, but no; I think I'm staying here.

Computer screens flash on and millions max
their credit cards again to make the rush
to get to "homes" that are and aren't ours,
and in the early dark, across black ice
and slushy snow, millions of wheels will spin
as they drift homeward for the holidays.

It's business

We now assume a playing field
with level ground and unconcealed

goals and borders, with a ref
who isn't on the take, or deaf.

But no such luck. The same old fix
against the rednecks from the sticks

still operates behind the bleachers,
admin halls, impassive features,

with club ties hidden under sweaters
so no one really knows one's "betters"

and cannot know the game's been thrown,
but thinks it's down to skill alone.

Suicide town

i.m. Ray Pospisil

Across the city, computer screens flash on—
in Brooklyn brownstones, littered sties of dorms,
Midtown offices, and Inwood flats.
Another day begins, a steely blue,
and we're above it, talking to ourselves
in tones of clacking keyboard strokes, our eyes
straining at the missives that we write
to cyberspace, expecting no reply.

Suicide town! Where unsung poets write
quarterly reports or articles
about the latest merger in Japan
or theses on the recent politics
of places that they fled to end up here—
bored, with just a screen for company.

New York, New York! Or Staten Island, Queens,
the Bronx, or Brooklyn, and far too many trains
with suicide lighting flickering on faces
until we look like corpses in the gloom,
pallid, with a laminate of sweat
glistening as we slump against the seats.

Sunset. Jersey glowers to the west.
Apartments echo a cacophony
of daydreams, words of love we only speak
into a pillow, and the tangled plots
of novels still unwritten, while our lives
are lived alone—and lonely—like a farce
without the comedy, until we slip,
drunk and murmuring, into our beds.

The rest of the story

There is no cause but this—a speeding train,
a damsel on the track. But it's not clear
why she was hog-tied as the train grew near,
or why the hero dashed across the plain,
all sweat and streaming hair. And did the villain
want her money, did he want revenge,
or what the hell's the story? Who will fill in
the damned ellipses? Therein lies the tinge
of bias, pious declarations, stock
melodrama, studies in archetype,
varying degrees of smut and hype,
specifics added in for added shock,
piano players plunking through a score
of tunes we know by heart, our certitude
the girl's, the hero's. He'll be back for more
next week, his hair in place, his methods crude.

Staying in

And, as in so much else, it all depends
on phones' staccato rings, or on the way
the new-cut grass looks from the street today.
In glossy magazines or calls to friends,
each blade in place is noted, with the ends
shorn neatly—and the reasons that we stay
are tidied up themselves; soft phrases sway
our sentiments. We make our tired amends.

Just staying in, it all falls into place
like forks and knives you line up side-to-side
or pillows not quite meeting on the bed—
or wrinkles working inward on your face,
an aching back, a reflex sense of pride,
and thoughts that never worm into your head.

The news comes every morning

Another day in waiting rooms. The doctor eyes the suture,
then bills you for a thousand bucks—says, "Think about the
          future."
The nurses smell of Calvin Klein, the waiting room of whiskey.
We stagger into taxicabs, our faces green and frisky.

I gave my love a cherry, and it floated in the cocktail.
We chatted till the bars were closed and broke it off by e-mail.
I gave my love a dining set. I gave my love a chicken.
She smothered it in flour and eggs, and so our waistlines thicken.

The news comes every morning, and the news is always bad.
The men on television smirk while slowly going mad.

A rumor spreads by radio, infecting like a virus
till counter-rumors put it down. It rises like Osiris,
twice as strong and tough as hell in its present incarnation.
I listened in a groggy haze, and then I switched the station.

We gave up dreams of second cars, of porches and cyclone fences,
of farting out the aftermath of coffee and cheese blintzes,
of jobs downtown and mortgages on houses in the valley—
all for a lurid fantasy of blowjobs in an alley.

The news comes every morning, but the morning's history
like pyramids, trench warfare, and the "new economy."

William Montgomery went to work, then blew his monthly
          paycheck
on a Nudie Cohen outfit made of sequins and white spandex.

Katie saw him and laughed so hard she gurgled through the
        bourbon
she sipped while she was driving home in her new gray Suburban.

Bill Clinton sucked—but didn't inhale—the tail end of a reefer,
served his time, serviced the girls, then floated into ether.
Hillary looked at the latest polls and threw away the paper.
"I might be sagging around the eyes, but at least I'm not Ralph
        Nader."

The news comes every morning, and the news is always brisk,
a ticker on the TV screen, a download saved to disk.

Someone's won a TV set; someone's won the Booker;
someone's won a million bucks on *Are You a Pirate Hooker?*
Someone's scared of rabid dogs; someone's scared of Satan;
someone's in his dad's garage, rocking to Van Halen.

You can crack equations; you can calculate the function
and end up scanning horoscopes for a distant star's conjunction.
You can buy insurance; you can keep away from matches;
but still, one day the lightning strikes and burns the place to ashes.

The only thing that changes is the light

We're back into the dream, on city streets
where sleepers mutter slogans as they sit
and pantomime a steering wheel while snoring
on a listless bus's upper deck.
The only thing that changes is the light.

The only thing that changes is the light
that permeates the mist we don't quite feel
though it cocoons the monuments and clothes
hanging, sodden, from our leaden limbs.
It's softer when we look from far away.

It's softer when we look from far away
and through improper lenses from an old
prescription made for slightly sharper eyes,
wide open and attentive to the flashes
blending into a glow as they recede.

Blending into a glow as they recede,
the stars dissolve to streetlights, headlights, night-lights.
We lip-synch history as we pass through
the thoroughfares that memory reroutes.
Familiar features alter into strangers'.

The only thing that changes is the light.
It's softer when we look from far away.
Blending into a glow as they recede,
familiar features alter into strangers'.

Less than expected

Take a breath, since this will hurt
a little less than you expect—
the promise of a trudge to work,
nights in front of the TV set,

an interest in the football match,
a furtive yearning for Miss June
that tingles upward from the crotch,
skin-rag eyes that beam disdain

though briefly, as the brain concocts
a minor victory, a spark
of sympathy that counteracts
unstated insults from the dark

that hum like crickets by the fence,
wordless in their creaking scorn,
allowing reason no defense
from accusations still half-formed

that rasp out what you never wished
while (mercifully) alone in bed,
fantasies that never washed,
the loss of what you never had.

Homelands

Homelands are overrated. As the surf
molded the hillside into newer shapes
I lay beside her, somewhere on the earth,
but two floors up. Tectonic plates may scrape
against each other, but the rumbling that I heard
wasn't an earthquake, but a foreign word
that spoke of this: her own geography,
visible in the moonlight that had crept
across the sheets, described in a litany
of places and events, and on the crest
of every jurisdiction was a slogan,
a promise made and then forgotten, broken
like treaties no one ever meant to honor.
And each assertion of who she thought she was
brought further strife, and by the dawn, her manner
was militant and hostile, as the Cause
demanded her allegiance and drove me out,
a foreigner, my loyalties in doubt.

Ye Watchers and Ye Holy Ones

Cold comfort, yes, that last descending line
that sinks into the rafters and the pews,
a seeming Pyrrhic triumph over death
that comes like backaches or the evening news
as we move on. A million lights will shine
against the empty sea.
                              We hold our breath,
or hold our loved ones. Cling with all our might!
Cling to unproven promises, the trust
that neither side has earned, although each must
preserve the proper forms and get it right.

Pause as the organ drones; the coalescence
of images and faces and abstraction
is broken by a cough, our very essence—
a sickly rasp, a faint, half-hearted action.

A fallacy, perhaps, and Lazarus
lies decomposed and stinking, while the stone
stays in its place. Neither alive nor dead,
we face that old uncertainty, alone
and in the outer darkness, each of us
pretending that we somehow hold the thread
that leads us out of here.
                              A murmured prayer
recalls a song and others who have passed
this way before. We wonder, at the last,
if other voices fill the rustling air.

The Year Zero

So try to catch a falling star,
Crush it into dust and stuff it down a jar
And throw it far away
—Mission of Burma, "Fame and Fortune"

I

Can we zero out the clock? Guitars
and drum and bass suggest the notion's dicey.
Despite the run-down surfaces of bars,
the beams below are new. The drinks are pricey.
But isn't there a look upon the faces
of trust-fund kids belying accusations
of simulacrum, summoning the traces
of lines erased some time ago? The notions
cross bounds of class and race and generations.
The kids are kids.

        We recognize the motions.
The DNA's unique, although it twists
the same old double helix, and the beat
seems to drive the blood inside our wrists
through bluish veins. The song will soon repeat
its chorus, though we can't hear every word.
And this is now, and everyone is young
and jumping up and down. It seems absurd
if you can't see it.

        Everything is new?
"We've see it all before"? Oh, have we really,
or something like it—Cabaret Voltaire,
Summer of Love? Tonight, the air is chilly,
but still, the dolled-up women's arms are bare,
trying to capture in a look the feel

129

of being where they are, but not quite here—
a place imagined, dropped into the real,
and trying to find a graft on fallow ground,
mutating with age and dressed in better gear.
Slogans fade. The rebels come around.

II

She loved to talk about her "art." I listened,
mouthed "Tristan Tzara," and she answered, "Who?"
The bar was hot; her unclad pale arms glistened.
Her eyes were painted. I said, "Siouxsie Sioux."
She stared at me a moment, turned away,
and chatted with her band about their label,
recording contracts, sessions in L.A.,
the audience (I gather we were fine).
The upward path is narrow and unstable.
Chaotic breaks become a chorus line.

I envied her that constant present tense,
that poise of ignorance, the sheer invention
of near-incompetence, her easy sense
of who she was, the arrogant pretension
that what you do's unique. And who was I
to stare her down with history, the hard
fact of antecedence, and a dry
account of revolutions that imploded,
the way the scions of the avant-garde
wake up one day, established and outmoded
or just washed up?

                    Fuck that! Get up on stage
until the money's gone, or till the spark
burns to an ember at an older age.
The backlit lights are bright. The tone is dark.
Rock on, young lady! (What the hell's her *name*?)
Stay right here, downstairs in a downtown bar.
Don't let them tell you that you're all the same.
Don't let me tell you who I think you are.

                            III

We've "seen it all before," the drunk flirtation
on the sidewalk, late nights on the streets,
the blank slate of a lack of reputation,
the flat with dirty dishes, dirty sheets,
and little space for second amplifiers
in the closet packed with piles of books,
a carpet of outdated concert fliers,
a girl more beautiful than you believe
—bewitching smile and slim exotic looks—
and noble notions, though perhaps naive.

But everything we take as read is new
for someone else still unendowed with loss,
the pessimism of the longer view,
the nature of the lines they have to cross.
Someday, they'll switch to khakis, though chagrined,
perhaps turned rueful at their indiscretions,
now smug and overpaid and double-chinned.
Or maybe they'll look back and smile that way
one does at some now-faded recollections
of what one used to be back in the day.

Brooklyn, 2008

I

We've plunged to winter. Economic graphs
   show more troughs than peaks
and promise further chills ahead
   in the coming weeks.
Sales are down. The stores are cutting prices,
   although to small avail.
Bills foreshadowing repo men
   show up in the mail.

Still, Christmas shoppers mill in Fulton Mall,
   and out in Prospect Park,
the yuppies follow happy dogs
   until the sky gets dark,
until the weather drops a bit too much,
   until the rent increases,
until the insurance won't pay up
   when faced with new diseases.

You'd think there'd have to be a protest march
   with banners—or a riot.
There's a light breeze in the Heights;
   in Park Slope, all seems quiet.
And only stops away in Williamsburg,
   the bars stay open late,
spilling out their bright young things
   in a fragile, altered state.

The psychiatric trade is always brisk.
   In little rooms, like priests,
they listen. We confess our sins,
   and for a time at least,

it's figured out, until the week's events
    circle to a chair
and soothing prints along the wall
    and a sympathetic stare.

And in that office, stammered sentences
    flow as the thoughts cohere—
the low-key power-plays at work,
    the shrapnel of a year
spent dodging each misfortune that arrives
    in this wave or the next—
company memos, budget cuts,
    the unmoved fairer sex.

Back on the subway, headphones set to stun
    echo with the crash
of waves of sound against the ear,
    quicker than the lash
of ebbs and flows of eyes that scan the ads
    plastered on the train.
Learn English! Start a New Career!
    Do You Suffer Pain?

But where's the toll-free number you can call
    when it gets cold and wet
or to check the status of a dream
    that's come to nothing yet?
The tide recedes into a half-read book,
    then breaks on strangers' faces,
back and forth, though we believe
    somehow, we're going places.

II

You're in a multiplex and wondering
   how it came to this—
beautiful people making love
   in cinematic bliss,
their shyness overcome. And all is grand
   until a second act
of obstacles soon overcome.
   You want your money back.

Back on the city street, it's still December.
   The sun's in short supply
as armies of overcoats go past.
   (The film's set in July.)
And somewhere, someone's working on a tan,
   and sometimes love's enough,
and someone's blonde, and someone's rich…
   but someone's life is rough,

and someone's house, foreclosed, is up for sale
   and someone's out of work.
A frenzied crowd has crushed the life
   out of a Walmart clerk,
trampled like a wrapper from a candy bar
   sticking to a shoe
as busy patrons rushed the shelves.
   What did you *think* they'd do?

Snarl at the cold and thrust a fist of coins
   at a gibbering bum,
get home, jerk off, and go to sleep
   before you, too, succumb

to the dissipation of a summer sky
    seen on celluloid.
The feeling lingers, though it shifts,
    soon to be redeployed.

And anyway, we all know what is what,
    and that the girls who grin
at you on platforms don't quite lie,
    but like their men more thin—
or muscular, or maybe not a stranger
    leaning against the glass.
They'll get off before your stop.
    Sigh. "This, too, shall pass."

It always passes, with the reassurance
    that she's "not your type,"
all mascara, heels, and blush,
    some bullshit market hype.
The "break-up," then, was strictly "mutual"
    —although you never spoke—
and never would have, anyway.
    She wouldn't like your jokes.

All the same, the luxury of scorn
    is some small blessing still,
a sign of better things to come,
    or maybe of "free will,"
a sense that we remain in some control
    of bank accounts and crushes
despite the crash of markets, and
    the squeeze of Christmas rushes.

III

Yesterday's headline: *Jobless Figures Surge.*
    The market's in a drought,
bringing on a greater thirst.
    Best spend the weekend out
and waffle on exhibits at the Met
    or recent politics,
post-it notes of conversation.
    Let's hope something sticks.

Friends and strangers sitting at the bar
    with ready, cutting quips
blend into the soundscape, till
    the jukebox CD skips,
and as a chord resounds *ad infinitum,*
    all the chatter stops.
The barman programs in a track.
    New song, from the top.

The women are all beautiful and bright;
    the men are fit and clever.
We'll all be plowed by closing time.
    For now, it holds together
like pop-song lyrics of *non sequiturs;*
    but isn't it "ironic,"
posing as poised and debonair
    with another gin and tonic?

Hangover. Just the standard easy fix
    of aspirin and food,
of diner coffee drunk in sips,
    the thought that life is good,

butter-soaked waffles, and a Spanish song
    with an upbeat refrain,
sustaining the smug certainty
    that you'll be here again.

And as the feeling lurking in the pain
    oozes out bit by bit,
you wonder why you do it, though
    nobody gives a shit—
and nor do you, despite the second thoughts
    that came, too late, at seven.
You've moved on to the sausages
    and swear that this is heaven.

We hurt because we can, not since we must—
    the difference is essential,
a fine distinction in the end
    but somehow fundamental
to all those bar tabs on the credit card,
    the freely flowing cash,
the love affair with the ATM,
    the mouth silted through with ash.

But as the headache dulls into a throb,
    the headline comes in clearer,
the same thing as the day before,
    ever so slightly nearer.
So take another aspirin and gulp
    your orange juice and pray
that the bill will not come due
    between now and Saturday.

IV

Bless the false dawn of a tunnel's gloom,
    the train just out of sight,
the blaze of headlights, the screech of brakes,
    the way our eyes alight
at the seemingly infernal glow.
    No. Blink. Expel the thought
like papers in a bin, a fleeting flash
    of details we forgot

somewhere between the bagel and the beer,
    between a boomed hello
and that goodbye we parted on.
    Stand up. It's time to go,
not into sunset or uncertain dawn,
    but (odd!) a sort of prayer,
chants mingling in a muted hum
    and lingering in the air.

We'll leave the train and start our ambles home
    in mobile meditation
as words congeal with clear intent
    but uncertain punctuation.
And if the phrases crumple into sound
    and ricochet off curbs
like rubbish tossed aside by drunks,
    we shouldn't be disturbed.

The night will give way soon enough to sounds
    of car alarms and voices
drowning out the subtler noise
    of our dubious choices

and second guesses of the two-room flats
    for which we pay the rent
or calculations of the cash
    waiting to be spent.

And blessed be you, despite this empty hour,
    wherever you might be—
awake in other time zones, or
    scant blocks away from me.
And if we haven't spoken, I recall
    an obsolete address.
I clutch the phone and pantomime
    the numbers that I'd press.

The number's doubted, leave it to tomorrow.
    Leave it *now,* full stop
and paragraph. Get through the door
    and take it from the top.
Brush your teeth; retreat into your bed,
    and think of gentler things—
the wondrous quiddity of day
    the morning always brings.

The context's staked out just beyond the door,
    a cop with an angry frown—
without a warrant, but still alert
    for when one's guard goes down.
Leave the thought unspoken, save in dreams
    that float out past the docks
like ships (or trash?) to far away—
    or founder on the rocks.

About the author

Quincy R. Lehr is a butt-scratching idiot who lives in Los Angeles and who despite a thoroughly nuked brain has had poems in such venues as *The Village Voice, The Dark Horse, Rattle, Barrow Street, The Orchards,* and *Measure.* He is the editor of *The Raintown Review,* and some day, he will own your skull.

www.ingramcontent.com/pod-product-compliance
Lightning Source LLC
Chambersburg PA
CBHW070332090426
42733CB00012B/2451